THAT'S MY JAM!

COUNTRY MUSIC

BY HEATHER E. SCHWARTZ

eureka!

EUREKA!, AN IMPRINT OF BELLWETHER MEDIA BY FLUTTERBEE

VHS

eureka!

Eureka! books turn real stories into unforgettable experiences. Clear, direct language and sharp, captivating imagery make it easy to follow your curiosity, one fascinating fact at a time.
Your Eureka! moment awaits!

This edition first published in 2027 by Bellwether Media, Inc.

Library of Congress Cataloging-in-Publication Data

Names: Schwartz, Heather E. author
Title: Country music / by Heather E. Schwartz.
Description: Eureka. | Minneapolis : Bellwether Media, Inc, 2027. | Series: That's my jam! | Includes index. | Audience: Ages 9-13 | Audience: Grades 7-9 | Summary: ""Engaging images accompany information on country music. The text level and subject matter are intended for students in grades 5 through 9"-Provided by publisher"-- Provided by publisher.
Identifiers: LCCN 2026016684 (print) | LCCN 2026016685 (ebook) | ISBN 9798898801236 (library binding) | ISBN 9798898802479 (ebook)
Subjects: LCSH: Country music--History and criticism
Classification: LCC ML3524 .S34 2027 (print) | LCC ML3524 (ebook) | DDC 782.421642--dc23/eng/20260327

LC record available at https://lccn.loc.gov/2026016684
LC ebook record available at https://lccn.loc.gov/2026016685

Editor: Ashley Kuehl Designer: Josh Brink

Printed in the United States of America, North Mankato, MN.

TABLE OF CONTENTS

WHAT IS COUNTRY?

Country music is famous for telling stories. Many songs focus on family life. Some are about romantic love. Others shine a light on problems. Faith is a common theme.

HILLBILLY

The word "hillbilly" refers to people in Appalachia. To some, the word is disrespectful. But many people there think it is positive.

Hillbilly is a type of country music. It keeps folk traditions alive. Bluegrass has a lonely sound. Country music features many instruments. They include banjos, fiddles, guitars, and harmonicas. Artists such as DeFord Bailey, Johnny Cash, and Dolly Parton created modern country music. They helped make it what it is today.

THE HISTORY OF COUNTRY

Country music has its roots in rural areas of the United States. But the people who started it came from other places. Some left England, Scotland, and Ireland to settle in the South. Others were taken from Africa and enslaved. They brought songs with them. Country music grew from these songs in the early 1900s.

GRAND OLE OPRY PERFORMANCE

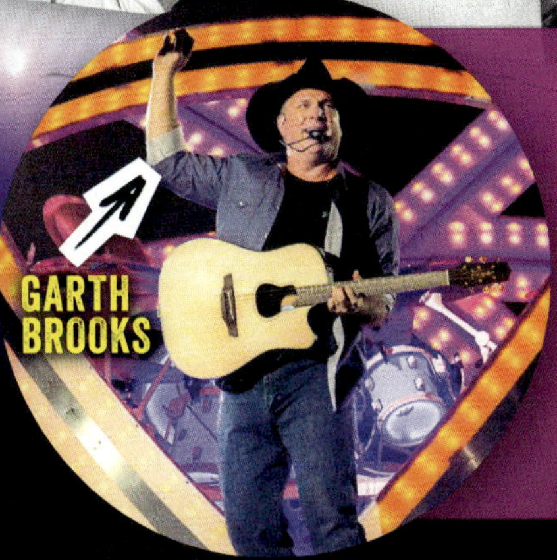

GARTH BROOKS

Nashville, Tennessee, is known for country music. That is because of the *Grand Ole Opry*. This radio show started with a barn dance. It was broadcast on the radio in 1925. Country was one of the first genres on the radio in the U.S. In 1974, the Opry House became a space for live performances. Modern superstars have played there. They include Taylor Swift, Darius Rucker, and Garth Brooks.

TAYLOR SWIFT

As more people learned about country music, it grew and changed. Different people tried different ideas. They brought in sounds from other cultures and genres. These included gospel, Cajun, rap, rock, R & B, and more. Willie Nelson became known for his jazz-style phrasing. The Charlie Daniels Band adopted electric fiddles.

WILLIE NELSON

RADIO PLAY

The Carter Family helped make country music popular. The band's recordings were played on the radio in the 1930s.

CHARLIE DANIELS

PETE SEEGER

WAYLON JENNINGS

New sounds and artists helped create new country styles. Folk artists Joan Baez and Pete Seeger helped inspire Americana. Waylon Jennings and Merle Haggard played outlaw country. This style moved away from what record labels wanted to hear. Country-rap grew starting in the 1990s. Artists mixed elements of hip-hop and country. Country music keeps changing.

JOAN BAEZ

MERLE HAGGARD

COUNTRY TIMELINE

1899
DeFord Bailey is born and later becomes the first Black country star

1924
The radio program the *National Barn Dance* begins broadcasting from Chicago

1925
The radio program the *Grand Ole Opry* begins broadcasting from Nashville

1927
The Carter Family begins to make hillbilly music popular

1955
Willie Nelson records his first two songs: "The Storm Has Just Begun" and "When I've Sung My Last Hillbilly Song"

WILLIE NELSON

CARTER FAMILY

1972

The Charlie Daniels Band forms, mixing sounds from folk, bluegrass, gospel, country, and rock

2010

Rhiannon Giddens records the bluegrass song "Cornbread and Butterbeans"

1960s

Waylon Jennings, Willie Nelson, Johnny Cash, and other artists begin to develop outlaw country

2019

Country-rap song "Old Town Road" by Lil Nas X and Billy Ray Cyrus tops the *Billboard* Hot 100 chart for 19 weeks

INSTRUMENTS

BANJO

Enslaved Africans invented the banjo in the 1600s. The earliest ones were made from gourds.

GOURD BANJO

FIDDLE (OR VIOLIN)

The first fiddle was created in Italy in the 1500s. It got people dancing. Immigrants brought the instrument to the U.S.

HARMONICA

The harmonica's history stretches back to China in 1100 BCE. Its modern design can be traced to 1780. By the 1820s, the instrument was small enough to carry around. It became popular through touring vaudeville shows.

1838 MARTIN

GUITAR

Christian Frederick Martin was a German immigrant. He made the first guitar with steel strings in the early 1900s. His invention made it easy to switch between banjo and guitar.

HARMONICA

AWARDS AND HONORS

THE CHICKS

COUNTRY MUSIC ASSOCIATION (CMA) AWARDS

The CMA began in Nashville in 1958. It was the first group devoted to a specific genre. Its awards show started in 1967.

GRAND OLE OPRY

The *Grand Ole Opry* began as a radio show in 1925. Fans can see live shows there. Top artists can be honored with membership.

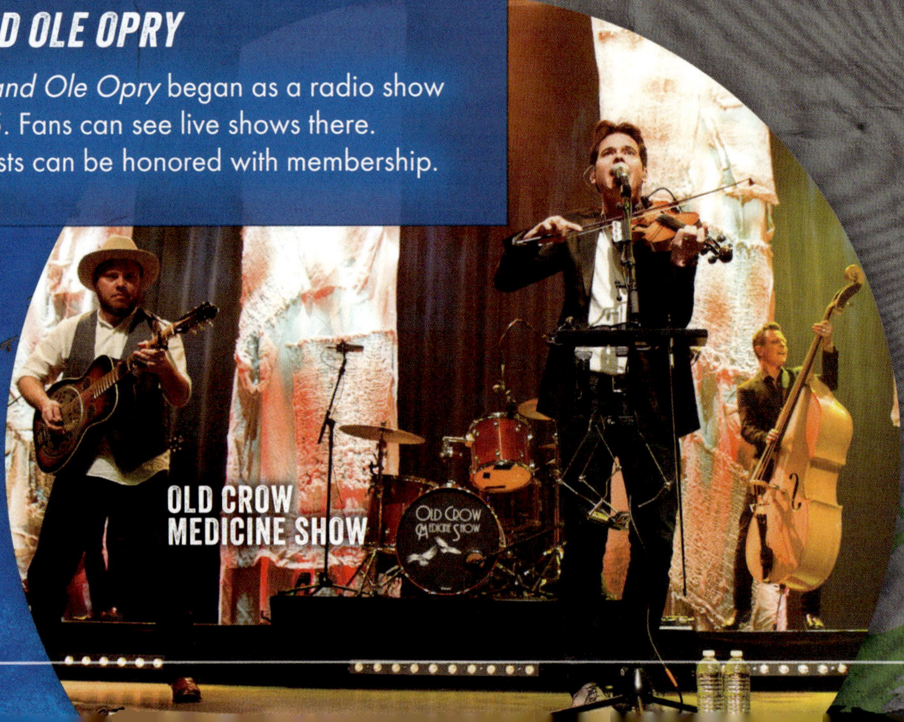

OLD CROW MEDICINE SHOW

SHABOOZEY

TAYLOR SWIFT

GRAMMY AWARDS

The Grammys began in 1959 to celebrate top musical artists. Top awards include Best New Artist, Song of the Year, Album of the Year, and Record of the Year.

ACADEMY OF COUNTRY MUSIC (ACM) AWARDS

The ACM was founded in 1964. It held its first awards show in 1966. It recognizes less traditional and more diverse modern country music.

CHRIS STAPLETON

TYPES OF COUNTRY

HILLBILLY

Date Started: 1920s

Traits:
- inspired by traditional hymns, folk music, and ballads
- passed down through generations
- includes a lot of fiddle and banjo

Song:
"Will You Miss Me When I'm Gone" by the Carter Family

WESTERN SWING

Date Started: late 1930s

Traits:
- heavy on stringed instruments and horns
- danceable rhythms
- jazz-based improvisation

Song:
"New Spanish Two-Step" by Bob Wills and the Texas Playboys

AMERICANA

Date Started: late 1940s

Traits:
- ◊ mixes bluegrass, roots-rock, folk, R & B, and blues
- ◊ often includes a mix of electric and acoustic instruments

Song: "The Devil Went Down to Georgia" by the Charlie Daniels Band

HONKY-TONK

Date Started: late 1940s

Traits:
- ◊ driving drumbeats
- ◊ edgy electric guitar
- ◊ sharp vocals that cut through crowd noise

Song: "Hey, Good Lookin'" by Hank Williams

BAKERSFIELD

Date Started: 1950s

Traits:
- ◊ driving beats
- ◊ electric guitars
- ◊ twangy sounds

Song:
"Stealin' Corn" by Merle Haggard and the Strangers

MERLE HAGGARD AND THE STRANGERS

BLUEGRASS

Date Started: 1940s

Traits:
- ◊ lonely-sounding string bands
- ◊ fast tempos
- ◊ high-pitched tones

Song:
"Cornbread and Butterbeans" by Rhiannon Giddens with Carolina Chocolate Drops

COUNTRYPOLITAN

Date Started: 1970s

Traits:
- smooth, soft sounds
- mixes country with pop
- less twangy than early country music

Song:
"Is Anybody Goin' to San Antone" by Charley Pride

OUTLAW COUNTRY

Date Started: 1960s

Traits:
- rock rhythms and undertones
- introspective lyrics
- quirky and nontraditional

Song:
"Hard to Be an Outlaw" by Billy Joe Shaver and Willie Nelson

COUNTRY-TRAP

Lil Nas X coined the term "country-trap." It describes his song "Old Town Road." The song combines country themes, banjo sounds, and rap and trap beats.

COUNTRY PROFILES

THE CARTER FAMILY

The Carter Family was a trio. It included A. P. Carter, Sara Dougherty Carter, and Maybelle Addington Carter. The group made traditional songs popular.

FORMING THE BAND

A. P. and Sara married in 1915. They played guitar, autoharp, and fiddle together. In 1926, Sara's cousin Maybelle joined them on guitar. Her special way of plucking strings became known as the "Carter lick." The Carter lick is still used today.

TIMELINE

1915
A. P. Carter marries Sara Dougherty

1926
Sara's cousin Maybelle joins their act

1927
They record their first songs together

Notable Members:
A. P. Carter,
Sara Dougherty Carter,
Maybelle Addington Carter

Place Formed:
Poor Valley, Virginia

Dates Active:
1926–1943

Type of Music:
hillbilly

First Hit Song:
"Keep on the Sunny Side"
(1928)

HUNDREDS OF SONGS

The Carter Family recorded their first songs in 1927. They soon recorded hundreds of songs. These included "Keep on the Sunny Side" and "Can the Circle Be Unbroken." In the 1930s, they were on the radio regularly.

HIT RELEASES

- ***The Original and Great Carter Family*** **(1962)**
- ***Three Generations*** **(1974)**
- ***The Essential Carter Family*** **(2013)**

1930s
The band plays regularly on the radio

1943
The Carter Family breaks up

PATSY CLINE

Patsy Cline was the first female solo artist to join the Country Music Hall of Fame.

ROUGH START

Cline's unhappy childhood made her want a better future. She wanted to be a singer. She landed her first recording contract in 1954. Her early songs were not popular. But she kept going.

RECOGNIZED TALENT

Cline's 1957 song "Walkin' After Midnight" was a success. She was inducted into the *Grand Ole Opry*. She appeared at Carnegie Hall. She was also on the TV show *American Bandstand*.

Birthday:
September 8, 1932

Death:
March 5, 1963

Hometown:
Winchester, Virginia

Type of Music:
Nashville

First Hit Song:
"Walkin' After Midnight" (1957)

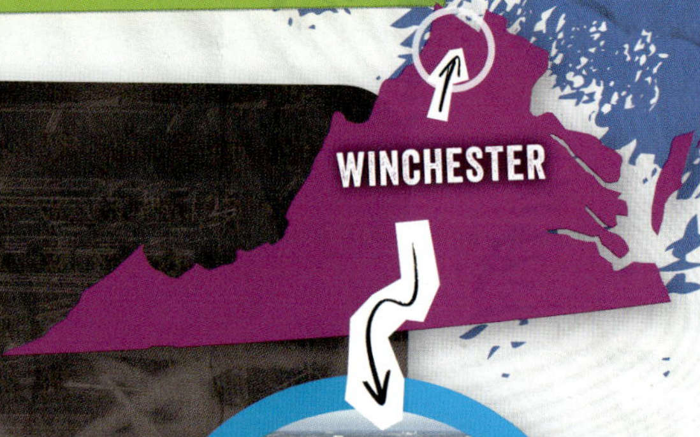

LASTING LEGACY

Cline died in a plane crash in 1963. She gave her last public performance just before she died. Her songs "Crazy" and "I Fall to Pieces" are still popular.

HIT RELEASES

- ***Patsy Cline*** **(1957)**
- ***Showcase*** **(1961)**
- ***Sentimentally Yours*** **(1962)**
- ***Live at the Opry*** **(1988)**
- ***Imagine That: The Lost Recordings (1954–1963)*** **(2025)**

TIMELINE

1954
Cline lands her first recording contract

1960
She becomes a member of the *Grand Ole Opry*

1961
She appears at Carnegie Hall

1962
She joins *The Johnny Cash Show*'s tour band as the star female vocalist

1963
She performs in public for the last time

JOHNNY CASH

Johnny Cash brought gospel and blues into the country sound.

MUSICAL MARRIAGE

Cash married musician June Carter. They performed together. June was the daughter of Maybelle Carter from the Carter Family.

LISTENING AND LEARNING

Cash grew up listening to gospel music at church. He heard country on the *Grand Ole Opry*. He learned to play guitar. In 1954, he formed a band. They got a record deal.

Birthday:
February 26, 1932

Death:
September 12, 2003

Hometown
Kingsland, Arkansas

Types of Music
gospel, blues, outlaw country

First Hit Songs:
"Cry! Cry! Cry!" and "Hey, Porter" (1955)

HIT RELEASES

I Walk the Line (1964)

At Folsom Prison (1968)

Hello, I'm Johnny Cash (1970)

Man in Black (1971)

A Thing Called Love (1972)

SHINING STAR

In 1969, Cash started hosting his own TV show, *The Johnny Cash Show*. He was voted the CMA Entertainer of the Year. In 2001, Cash was honored with the National Medal of Arts.

PERSONAL TOUCH

Cash wrote most of his own songs. They were very personal. His song "I Walk the Line" and many others were beloved among pop and country fans. His work spread the country sound.

TIMELINE

1955
Cash gets his first record deal

1956
Cash records "I Walk the Line," which becomes his first number one single

1969
He starts hosting *The Johnny Cash Show* on TV

1969
He is voted the CMA Entertainer of the Year

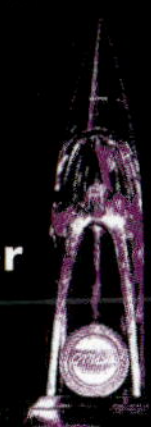

2001
He wins the National Medal of Arts

WILLIE NELSON

Willie Nelson is one of country's most prolific songwriters. He has written more than 300 songs.

EARLY EXPLORATIONS

Nelson grew up listening to many types of music. He played in polka bands.

HIT RELEASES

Red Headed Stranger **(1975)**

Stardust **(1978)**

Always On My Mind **(1982)**

City of New Orleans **(1984)**

Band of Brothers **(2014)**

TRIGGER

In 1969, Nelson bought a guitar. He named it Trigger. It grew worn and battered. Nelson still plays it today.

RISING STAR

Nelson moved to Nashville in 1960. He signed his first major label recording contract two years later. He became a member of the *Grand Ole Opry*. He started acting too. In 1980, he starred in the movie *Honeysuckle Rose*.

TIMELINE

1960 Nelson moves to Nashville

1962 Nelson signs his first major label recording contract

1964 He becomes a member of the *Grand Ole Opry*

CULTURE CREATOR

Many songs Nelson wrote are part of American culture. "On the Road Again" is one. Another is "Crazy," made famous by Patsy Cline. In 2012, the CMA created the Willie Nelson Lifetime Achievement Award.

Birthday:
April 29, 1933

Hometown:
Abbott, Texas

Types of Music:
honky-tonk, outlaw country

First Hit Songs:
"Touch Me" and "Willingly" (1962)

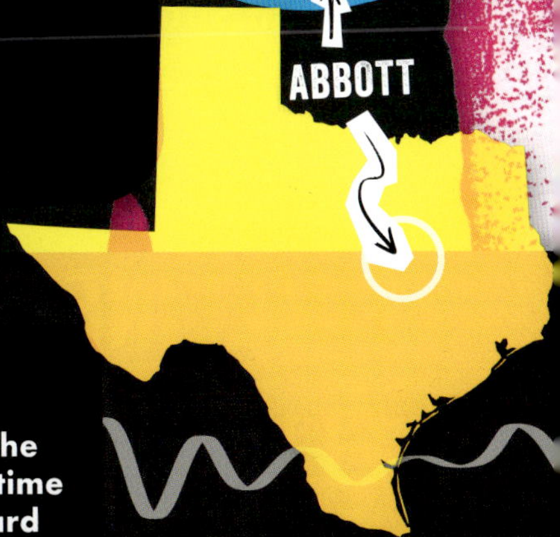

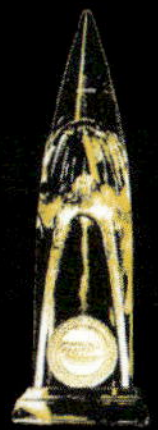

1980
He stars in the movie *Honeysuckle Rose*

2012
The CMA creates the Willie Nelson Lifetime Achievement Award

FREDDY FENDER

Freddy Fender was a Mexican American pop-country star. His career lasted five decades.

TRAVELING SOUNDS

Fender's parents were migrant farm workers. The family traveled for work. Other workers were talented blues musicians. These sounds became part of Fender's music style. Fender played pop, country, and Tejano music. Tejano is a Mexican American genre. It started in southern Texas.

Birthday:
June 4, 1937

Death:
October 14, 2006

Hometown:
San Benito, Texas

Types of Music:
Tejano, pop, country

First Hit Song:
"Before the Next Teardrop Falls" (1974)

TIMELINE

1947
Fender first performs on the radio at age 10

1957
Fender releases two hit songs in Mexico and South America as the Bebop Kid

1975
"Before the Next Teardrop Falls" hits number one on both the *Billboard* pop and country charts

SPANISH SINGER

Fender played Spanish versions of popular English songs. He covered Elvis Presley and Harry Belafonte. He wrote his own songs too. He sang in both English and Spanish.

TEX-MEX GROUPS

Later on, Fender joined two bands. The Texas Tornados and Los Super Seven both won Grammys.

HIT RELEASES

- ***Before the Next Teardrop Falls*** (1974)
- ***Are You Ready for Freddy?*** (1975)
- ***Rock 'N' Country*** (1976)
- ***Swamp Gold*** (1978)
- ***La Musica de Baldemar Huerta*** (2002)

IN A NAME

Fender took his name from the Fender guitar. He liked how Freddie sounded with it. He thought the name would appeal to white listeners.

1989
Fender joins the Texas Tornados

2002
Fender's solo album *La Musica de Baldemar Huerta* wins a Grammy

DOLLY PARTON

Dolly Parton is a popular singer and songwriter. She is also a philanthropist.

CHILD STAR

Parton grew up poor. But she had a large, loving family. Her uncle bought her a guitar. She appeared on the *Grand Ole Opry* at age 13.

Dollywood

GIVING BACK

In 1988, Parton formed the Dollywood Foundation. The charity has given scholarships. It has helped families who lost their homes to fires. It has also donated millions of books.

Birthday:
January 19, 1946

Hometown:
Locust Ridge, Tennessee

Types of Music:
bluegrass, pop

First Hit Song:
"Dumb Blonde" (1966)

LIFE STORIES

Parton has an emotional singing style. Her songs tell stories from her life. In 1975, she won the CMA Female Vocalist of the Year Award. In 1980, she starred in the movie *9 to 5*. She started her own record label in 2007. It is called Dolly Records.

TRIPLE TALENT

Parton won a Lifetime Achievement Award in 2011. The award honored her work as an artist, songwriter, and performer.

HIT RELEASES

Coat of Many Colors **(1971)**

My Tennessee Mountain Home **(1973)**

Jolene **(1974)**

Here You Come Again **(1977)**

Trio **(1987)**

TIMELINE

1959
Parton first appears on the *Grand Ole Opry*

1975
She wins the CMA Female Vocalist of the Year Award

1980
She stars in the movie *9 to 5*.

2007
She starts her own record label, Dolly Records

2022
She is inducted into the Rock & Roll Hall of Fame

LORETTA LYNN

Loretta Lynn was a voice for women and working-class people.

TOUGH BEGINNING

Lynn grew up poor. She got married at 15. She taught herself to play guitar. Soon, Lynn began performing. She released her first record in 1960. She played at the *Grand Ole Opry*.

Birthday:
April 14, 1932

Death:
October 4, 2022

Hometown:
Butcher Holler, Kentucky

Type of Music:
honky-tonk

First Hit Song:
"I'm a Honky Tonk Girl" (1960)

TIMELINE

1960
Lynn releases her first record and appears on the *Grand Ole Opry*

1972
She becomes the first woman to receive the CMA Entertainer of the Year award

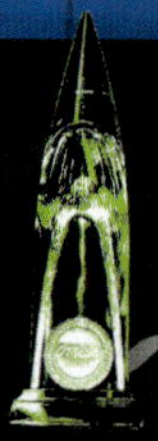

1980
Her autobiography, *Coal Miner's Daughter*, is made into a movie

WINNING WOMAN

In 1972, she was the first woman to receive the CMA Entertainer of the Year Award. Her autobiography was made into a movie in 1980. She released her 46th album, *Still Woman Enough*, in 2021.

HIT RELEASES

- ***Loretta Lynn Sings*** (1963)
- ***You Ain't Woman Enough*** (1966)
- ***Somebody Somewhere*** (1976)
- ***Just a Woman*** (1985)
- ***Van Lear Rose*** (2004)

PAVING THE WAY

Lynn's songs told personal stories. She wrote about social problems. She created a path for female artists to speak up and be heard.

2010
Lynn receives a Grammy Lifetime Achievement Award

2021
She releases her 46th album, *Still Woman Enough*

CHARLEY PRIDE

Charley Pride won many country music awards. He had 29 number one songs on the *Billboard* Hot Country chart.

VARIED INTERESTS

Pride grew up on a cotton farm. He played baseball. He also listened to the *Grand Ole Opry*. He taught himself to play guitar at 14. He later played baseball in the Negro American League.

DIALING IN

In 1965, Pride recorded his first songs in Nashville. In 1971, he was the CMA Entertainer of the Year. He was inducted into the *Grand Ole Opry* in 1993.

BREAKING BARRIERS

Linda Martell was a Black country star. Like Charley Pride, she performed in the 1970s. She quit music because of racism she faced. In 2024, Martell worked with Beyoncé on the *COWBOY CARTER* album.

Birthday:
March 18, 1934

Death:
December 12, 2020

Hometown:
Sledge, Mississippi

Types of Music:
honky-tonk, countrypolitan

First Hit Song:
"Just Between You and Me" (1966)

PUSHING FORWARD

Pride faced discrimination. The record label kept his race a secret. They did not reveal it until his album *Country Charley Pride* became popular. Pride made way for future Black country singers. He helped them gain both success and respect.

HIT RELEASES

- *Country Charley Pride* (1966)
- *Just Plain Charley* (1970)
- *Charley Pride Sings Heart Songs* (1971)
- *The Happiness of Having You* (1975)
- *After All This Time* (1987)

TIMELINE

1950s
Pride plays baseball in the Negro American League

1965
Pride records his first songs in Nashville

1971
He wins the CMA Entertainer of the Year award

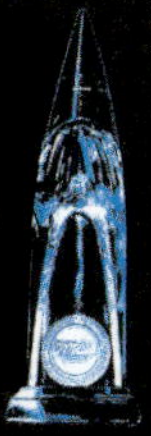

1993
He becomes the first Black musician inducted into the *Grand Ole Opry*

2000
He is inducted into the Country Music Hall of Fame

EMMYLOU HARRIS

Emmylou Harris is a singer, songwriter, and guitarist. Her creativity has transformed country music.

FAVORING FOLK

Harris loved folk songs growing up. Her first recording was a folk album called *Gliding Bird*. In 1975, she released her first solo country album. It was called *Pieces of the Sky*.

CREATIVE COLLABORATIONS

Harris loves working with other artists. She has discovered new songwriters and formed bands. In 1987, she recorded *Trio* with Linda Ronstadt and Dolly Parton. She joined the *Grand Ole Opry* in 1992.

Birthday:
April 2, 1947

Hometown:
Birmingham, Alabama

Types of Music:
folk, country rock

First Hit Song:
"If I Could Only Win Your Love" (1975)

HIT RELEASES

- *Pieces of the Sky* (1975)
- *Luxury Liner* (1976)
- *At the Ryman* (1992)
- *Wrecking Ball* (1995)
- *Stumble into Grace* (2003)

PAST AND PRESENT

Harris balances both history and the future in her work. She has brought a modern style and sound to traditional country music.

FURRY FRIENDS

In 2004, Harris founded Bonaparte's Retreat. It finds homes for senior dogs and dogs that have medical needs.

TIMELINE

1969
Harris releases a folk album called *Gliding Bird*

1975
She releases her first solo country album, *Pieces of the Sky*

1987
She records the album *Trio* with Linda Ronstadt and Dolly Parton

1992
She becomes a member of the *Grand Ole Opry*

2008
She is inducted into the Country Music Hall of Fame

DARIUS RUCKER

Darius Rucker is a pop star turned country star. He has Grammys in both genres.

TOP IN POP

Rucker grew up singing in church and his high school choir. He and his college friends formed the band Hootie & the Blowfish. They wrote many popular songs. "Hold My Hand" and "I Only Want to Be with You" were big hits.

CHART TOPPER

Rucker's song "Don't Think I Don't Think About It" topped the *Billboard* Hot Country Songs chart in July 2008. The last Black singer to hit this milestone was Charley Pride in 1983.

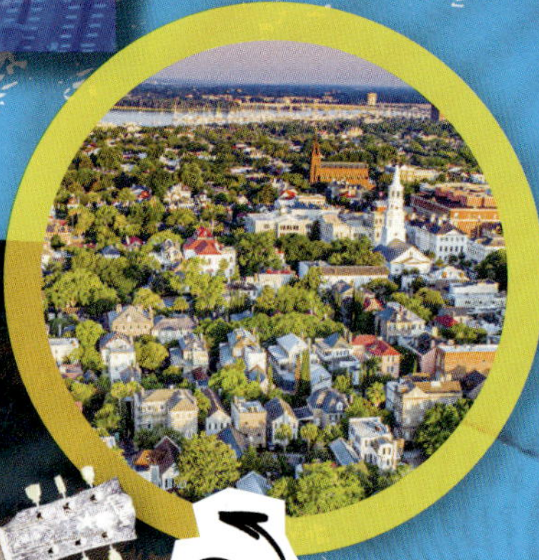

Birthday:
May 13, 1966

Hometown:
Charleston, South Carolina

Types of Music:
pop, R & B, country

First Hit Song:
"Don't Think I Don't Think About It" (2008)

TURNING COUNTRY

In 1998, Rucker started his solo career in country music. He played at the *Grand Ole Opry* in 2008. He also released *Learn to Live* that year.

PIONEERING ARTIST

Rucker brings sincerity, passion, and diversity to pop and country. His success as a Black artist has paved the way for other artists of color.

HIT RELEASES

- ***Cracked Rear View*** **(1994)**
- ***Learn to Live*** **(2008)**
- ***Southern Style*** **(2015)**
- ***When Was the Last Time*** **(2017)**

TIMELINE

1986
Rucker and his friends form the band Hootie & the Blowfish

1998
He starts working on his solo career

2008
Rucker plays at the *Grand Ole Opry*

2008
He releases the country album *Learn to Live*

2023
He releases his sixth country album, *Carolyn's Boy*

AMYTHYST KIAH

Amythyst Kiah is breaking new ground as a Black LGBTQ+ artist.

STAR STUDENT

Kiah had musical parents. She taught herself to play guitar. She studied blues, old time, and country music in college.

CAREER BUILDER

Kiah started touring in 2010. She released her first album, *Dig*, in 2013. In 2018, she started performing with the group Our Native Daughters. Kiah describes her music as "Southern Gothic." It combines storytelling with both strange and familiar sounds.

TIMELINE

2010
Kiah begins touring

2013
She releases her first album, *Dig*

2016
She releases *Chest of Glass*

BREAKING BOUNDARIES

Kiah debuted at the *Grand Ole Opry* in 2021. She is challenging ideas about who belongs in country music. She offers a new twist on how it sounds and the kinds of stories it can tell.

REVIVING STORIES

Our Native Daughters includes Kiah, Rhiannon Giddens, Leyla McCalla, and Allison Russell. The group revived stories of Black people who were enslaved in the U.S.

HIT RELEASES

Dig
(2013)

Songs of Our Native Daughters
(2019)

Wary + Strange
(2021)

Still + Bright
(2024)

Birthday:
December 11, 1986

Hometown:
Chattanooga, Tennessee

Type of Music:
alt-country

First Hit Song:
"Your Ghost" (2020)

2018
She and other musicians form the group Our Native Daughters

2021
She debuts at the *Grand Ole Opry*

LAINEY WILSON

Lainey Wilson brings classic country music to a modern audience.

STARTING YOUNG

Wilson grew up dancing with her sister to their dad's guitar playing. She wrote her first song when she was nine. She started playing guitar two years later.

HIT RELEASES

Tougher
(2016)

Redneck Hollywood
(2019)

Bell Bottom Country
(2022)

Whirlwind
(2024)

HANNAH MONTANA

As a teenager, Wilson worked as an impersonator. She sang as Disney TV character Hannah Montana. She played at birthday parties, hospitals, and more.

TIMELINE

2011
Wilson moves to Nashville at age 19

2021
Wilson releases "WWDD (What Would Dolly Do)," a tribute to Dolly Parton

2022
Wilson wins her first two CMAs

MULTITALENTED

Wilson is an actor too. She has been on TV and film. She played a musician on the TV show *Yellowstone*. It helped her career.

Birthday:
May 19, 1992

Hometown:
Baskin, Louisiana

Types of Music:
contemporary country, country pop

First Hit Song:
"Things a Man Oughta Know" (2020)

2022
Wilson acts on the TV series *Yellowstone*

2024
***Bell Bottom Country* wins a Grammy for Best Country Album**

THE FUTURE OF COUNTRY

CARRIE UNDERWOOD

Country music has always been a mix of styles and sounds. Modern favorites include Chris Stapleton and Carrie Underwood. Megan Moroney and Bailey Zimmerman are rising stars.

CHRIS STAPLETON

ALISON NICHOLS

MEGAN MORONEY

Nigerian-American Shaboozey mixes Americana with hip-hop. Asian-American artists Alison Nichols and Travis Yee are on the rise. So are Mexican American artists such as Louie TheSinger. Some artists are making country music in other languages. South Korea's Country GongBang combines bluegrass and K-pop.

BEYONCÉ

POST MALONE

JELLY ROLL

Artists in other genres make country music too. Beyoncé, Jelly Roll, and Post Malone have released country albums. Each new voice, style, and sound has something to contribute. They build on traditions. And they bring country music into the future.

LOUIE THESINGER

BAILEY ZIMMERMAN

GLOSSARY

acoustic—sounds or instruments created without the help of electronics

autoharp—a musical instrument played using strings and buttons

ballads—slow, sentimental, or romantic songs

broadcast—played on the radio or television

cultures—the beliefs, arts, and ways of life in a place or society

debuted—first appeared

discrimination—the act of treating someone unfairly because of race, gender, age, or other differences

diverse—showing a lot of variety

enslaved—thought of as property and forced to work without pay

genres—categories for types of music

gourds—large fruits with hard skins

impersonator—a performer who plays the role of a famous entertainer

inducted—to be officially admitted as a member of an organization

inspire—give someone an idea about what to do or create

introspective—looking inward to one's own thoughts and feelings

LGBTQ+—a community of people who identifies as something other than heterosexual or the gender they were assigned at birth; LGBTQ+ stands for Lesbian, Gay, Bisexual, Transgender, Queer, and other identities.

philanthropist—a person who seeks to help others, especially by donating money to good causes

phrasing—the way a singer or musician shapes a passage of musical notes with emotion

prolific—productive and creative

rhythms—strong, regular, repeated patterns of movement or sound

rural—related to the country or countryside

scholarships—money to support a student's education

tempos—the speeds at which music is played

tones—musical sounds related to pitch, quality, and strength

traditions—ways of doing things that have been done for a long time

twangy—nasal vocal sounds; harsh, ringing string sounds.

undertones—low, secondary sounds

vaudeville—a type of entertainment popular in the early 1900s featuring acts such as comedy, song, and dance

WRITE ABOUT IT!

- Which artist do you think has had the biggest impact on country music? **Why?**
- What are some of your favorite country songs? **Why do you like them?**
- How do you think country music will continue to **change** in the future?

ALSO CHECK OUT

INDEX

The images in this book are reproduced through the courtesy of: Gorodenkoff, front cover (hero); Wesley C.D, front cover (fiddle); AnnaStills, front cover (bass); Ben Houdijk, front cover (banjo); CBS Photo Archive/ Contributor/ Getty Images, pp. 3 (Johnny Cash), 4 (Johnny Cash), 24 (bottom left), 24-25 (Johnny Cash), 25 (bottom), 26 (top); Hulton Archive/ Staff/ Getty Images, pp. 3 (Loretta Lynn), 33 (Loretta Lynn); Rob Verhorst/ Contributor/ Getty Images, pp. 3 (Charley Pride), 34-35 (Charley Pride); Marilyn K. Morton/ Wikimedia Commons, p. 4 (Deford Bailey); CREATISTA, pp. 4-5 (banjo); Lone Star Stock, p. 5 (fiddle); Kevin Mazur/ Contributor/ Getty Images, pp. 5 (Dolly Parton), 11 (2019); MakingMovesPhotography, p. 5 (hillbilly); Terry Wyatt/ Stringer/ Getty Images, pp. 6 (Darius Rucker), 41 (top); A.PAES, pp. 6-7; Bob Grannis/ Contributor/ Getty Images, p. 7 (top); Sterling Munksgard, pp. 7 (middle), 8 (top), 14 (bottom), 26 (bottom), 44 (middle); Michael Ochs Archives/ Stringer/ Getty Images, pp. 8 (middle), 10 (1955), 11 (1960s), 16 (top), 17 (left), 18-19, 19 (top), 21 (middle right), 22-23, 26 (middle), 34 (middle left); Tim Mosenfelder/ Contributor/ Getty Images, pp. 8 (bottom), 28 (bottom left); Sulfiati Magnuson/ Contributor/ Getty Images, pp. 8-9; Donna Lou Morgan, U.S. Navy/ Wikimedia Commons, p. 9 (top left); Larry Hulst/ Contributor/ Getty Images, p. 9 (top right); Paul Natkin/ Contributor/ Getty Images, p. 9 (bottom right); American Broadcasting Company-ABC/ Wikimedia Commons, p. 10 (1924); Victor Talking Machine Company/ Wikimedia Commons, p. 10 (1927); Olga Steckel, p. 11 (1972); Carl Beust, p. 11 (2010); Thomas Quine/ Wikimedia Commons, p. 11 (top left); Alexander Image, p. 12 (top right); Arthur Villator, p. 12 (bottom); Dimensions, p. 13 (top); cogito ergo imago/ Wikimedia Commons, p. 13 (middle left); Denis Ivatin, p. 13 (middle right); Tony Norkus, p. 13 (bottom); Featureflash Photo Agency, pp. 14 (top), 37 (top), 42 (top); s_bukley, pp. 14 (CMA), 15 (top right), 25 (CMA), 27 (CMA), 31 (CMA), 35 (CMA); Leon Bennett/ Stringer/ Getty Images, p. 15 (top left); Bernd Schwabe/ Wikimedia Commons, pp. 15 (Grammy), 33 (Grammy); Kathy Hutchins, pp. 15 (bottom left, bottom right), 30 (middle left); Archiv PL/ Alamy Stock Photo, p. 16 (bottom); Taylor Hill/ Contributor/ Getty Images, p. 17 (right); Ebet Roberts/ Contributor/ Getty Images, pp. 18 (left), 19 (bottom); Benoît Prieur/ Wikimedia Commons, p. 20 (left); Donaldson Collection/ Contributor/ Getty Images, pp. 20 (right), 21 (bottom); Lefteris Papaulakis, p. 21 (top); Michael Sledjeski/ Wikimedia Commons, p. 21 (middle left); Ritu Manoj Jethani, pp. 22 (top), 30 (top right), 37 (2008); Shanecollinswiki, p. 22 (middle); Richard Weize/ Contributor/ Getty Images, p. 22 (bottom left); Reagan, p. 22 (bottom right); ZUMA Press, Inc./ Alamy Stock Photo, pp. 23 (top), 30 (middle right); Dr. Blazer, p. 24 (bottom right); Panther Media Global/ Alamy Stock Photo, p. 25 (top); TaurusEmerald/ Wikimedia Commons, p. 25 (2001); Ga Fullner, p. 27 (top right); Tom Hill/ Contributor/ Getty Images, p. 27 (middle left); Ron Galella, Ltd./ Contributor/ Getty Images, p. 27 (middle right); Josh Withers, p. 27 (bottom left); Renelibrary/ Wikimedia Commons, p. 27 (bottom right; Falcon Records/ Wikimedia Commons, p. 28 (top); Graham Bezant/ Contributor/ Getty Images, p. 28 (bottom right); David Redfern/ Staff/ Getty Images, pp. 28-29; Gene Pugh/ Wikimedia Commons, p. 29 (left); bergamont, p. 29 (bottom); PA Images/ Contributor/ Getty Images, pp. 30-31; Joseph Hendrickson, p. 30 (left); Harry Langdon/ Contributor/ Getty Images, p. 30 (bottom left); Bart Sherkow, p. 30 (bottom right); RCA Records/ Wikimedia Commons, pp. 31 (middle), 35 (middle); Adam Shanker, p. 31 (bottom); 3DMI, p. 31 (2022); Debby Wong, pp. 32 (top left), 32 (middle right); CBS Television/ Wikimedia Commons, p. 32 (top right); Johnnie Laws, p. 32 (middle left); Nicolai Edgar Andersen/ Wikimedia Commons, p. 3 (middle); Michael Ochs Archives/ Handout/ Getty Images, p. 33 (bottom); GREG MATHISON/ Wikimedia Commons, p. 34 (top left); Joe Seer, p. 34 (top right); Frederick Breedon/ Stringer/ Gett Images, p. 34 (middle); Magnolia677/ Wikimedia Commons, p. 34 (middle right); Silver Screen Collection/ Contributor/ Getty Images, p. 34 (bottom); Marcus E Jones, p. 35 (2000); Rob Bogaerts/ Anefo/ Wikimedia Commons, p. 36 (left); Dan Reeder/ Contributor/ Getty Images, p. 36 (bottom left); BJ Ray, p. 36 (bottom right); chris87, pp. 36-37; Everett Collection, p. 37 (bottom); Eugene Parciasepe, p. 38 (top left); Mysti Cabasug, U.S. Air Force/ Wikimedia Commons, p. 38 (top right); Gary Miller/ Contributor/ Getty Images, p. 38 (middle left); Kevin Ruck, pp. 38 (middle right), 41 (bottom); Michael Bush, p. 38 (bottom); Starstock, p. 39 (left); Mickey Bernal/ Stringer/ Getty Images, p. 39 (right); RICHARD PIERRIN/ Contributor/ Getty Images, p. 4 (top); Mickey Bernal/ Contributor/ Getty Images, p. 40 (bottom); Erika Goldring/ Contributor/ Getty Images, pp. 40-41; Scott Dudelson/ Contributor/ Getty Images, p. 41 (middle); Terry Wyatt Contributor/ Getty Images, pp. 42-43; Jason Kempin/ Staff/ Getty Images, p. 43 (top); Helloburton, p. 43 (middle); Ed Rode/ Stringer/ Getty Images, p. 43 (bottom left); AFF, p. 43 (bottom right); MPH Photos, p. 44 (top); Geoffrey Clowes, p. 44 (bottom left); Evan Agostini/ Invision/ AP Images, p. 44 (bottom right); Alex Slitz/ Staff/ Getty Images, p. 45 (top); Harvey Aspell, p. 45 (middle left); Howard Weiss, p. 45 (middle right); Timothy Norris/ Contributor/ Getty Images, p. 45 (bottom left); BrDen/ Wikimedia Commons, p. 45 (bottom right).